The Story of Easter

ISBN-13: 978-0-8249-5560-1
ISBN-10: 0-8249-5560-9

Published by Ideals Children's Books
An imprint of Ideals Publications
A Guideposts Company
535 Metroplex Drive, Suite 250
Nashville, Tennessee 37211
www.idealsbooks.com

Color separations by Precision Color Graphics, Franklin, Wisconsin

Printed and bound in Italy by LEGO

Library of Congress Cataloging-in-Publication Data on file

10 9 8 7 6 5 4 3 2 1

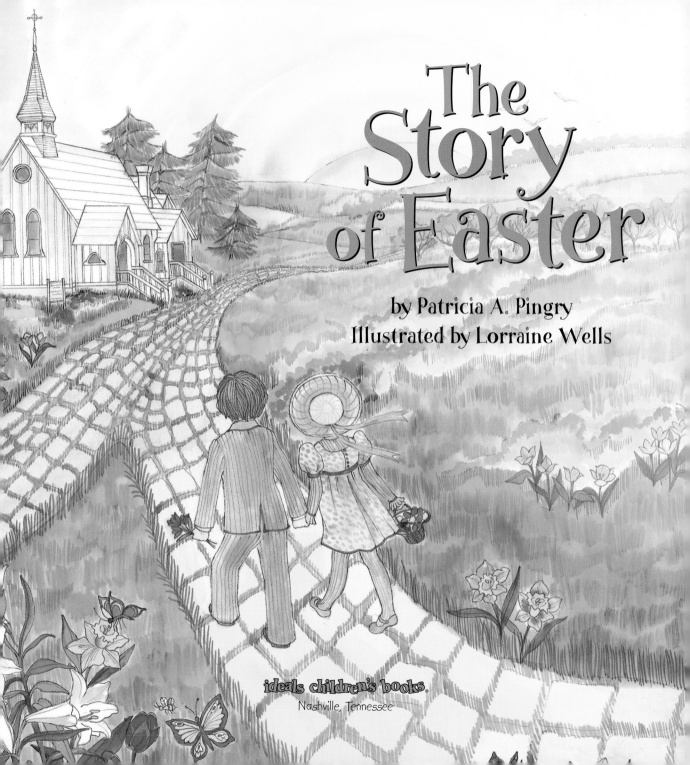

The Story of Easter

by Patricia A. Pingry

Illustrated by Lorraine Wells

ideals children's books.
Nashville, Tennessee

When spring
comes, baby
animals are born,
and flowers
begin to bloom.

Springtime
also brings Easter.
On Easter we
remember
Jesus and what
He did for us.

Jesus
loved all
boys and girls,
and moms
and dads too.
He was called the
Good Shepherd.

Moms and dads
and boys and
girls loved
Jesus, too.
They laid palm
branches in
His path.

But some men
did not like
Jesus.
They put Him
on a cross to die.
His friends
were sad.

On that first
Easter, Jesus'
friends met
an angel.
He told them,
"Jesus has risen!
He is alive today!"
His friends were
very happy.

We celebrate
Easter because
Jesus lived again
on that first
Easter morning.

On Easter
Sunday we go
to church and
sing about Jesus.

Churches
place crosses
on their
steeples
to remind us
of Jesus' love.

Now on Easter
morning you'll
know that Jesus
loved us so
much that . . .

He gave His
life for us
so that we
can live too.